KB244200

Tales from the Talmud

Happy House

About Wise & Wide

- A systematic 6-level English reading program based on Lexile® measures
- Diverse and interesting topics chosen from the elementary curriculums of Korea and English speaking western countries
- Well-written books in various forms including fiction stories, descriptive texts, and classics retold
- The informative but original fiction stories grab your interest, leading to the easy and clear understanding of the educational content.
- Improve thinking skills with solid after-reading activities at all levels of the series.

Wise & Wide is a 6-level English reading program that consists of 60 books and each level is systematically divided by Lexile® measures. The Lexile® Framework for Reading is the most popular reading measuring system in American formal education curriculums and many English programs. Over 20 out of 50 states in the U.S. mark Lexile® measures directly on students' final report cards and over 300 well-known publishers adopt and use Lexile® measures.

Experience many kinds of readings written by professional writers from the U.S. and England. They used interesting topics that were carefully chosen after analyzing elementary curriculums from around the world including Korea, the U.S., England, and Australia among many others. Comprehensive after-reading activities including graphic organizers, speaking tasks, and After-reading Tests are ready for you.

Levels in the series and their corresponding Lexile® measures

Level	Lexile® measures	U.S. Grade
Level 1	Below 200L	Pre K - K
Level 2	190L - 400L	Lower Grade 1
Level 3	350L - 530L	Upper Grade 1
Level 4	420L - 650L	Grade 2
Level 5	520L - 940L	Grade 3 - 4
Level 6	830L - 1070L	Grade 5 - 6

* Smart Readers: Wise & Wide level 1 is applicable to the preschool level in the U.S.

* The source of the relationship between Lexile® measures and U.S. school grades: CCSS(Common Core State Standards) FOR ENGLISH LANGUAGE ARTS, APPENDIX A (2012, which is used by 45 states in the U.S.)

Topic List

	Level 1	Level 2	Level 3	Level 4	Level 5	Level 6
Book 1	Science>Biology: The hibernation of animals Story	Science>Biology: Living and nonliving things Story	Science>Biology> Animals & the Environment: Sea otters Story	Environment> Living with nature: The diver & the persimmon tree Story	Science>Biology> Animal: Amazing animals of the Amazon Story	Science>Biology: Germs, transmitted diseases Story
Book 2	Literature> World classics: Aesop's fables Story	Literature> Traditional fairy tale: Old tales about stones Story	Social Studies> Economy: To run a business to make and save money Story	Science>Biology> Plants: Photosynthesis Story	Science>Earth science: Earth's layers, earthquakes, volcanoes, and earth's atmosphere Report	Mathematics> Sequence: The golden ratio & the Fibonacci sequence Story
Book 3	Science>Physics: How shadows are formed Story	Literature> World classics: Peter Pan Story	Science>Scientific technology: Nanobots Story	Literature>Myths: World's creation stories Story	Literature> Legend: The story of King Arthur Story	Literature>Myths: Constellation myths Story
Book 4	Literature> Traditional literature: The Talmud Story	Science>Biology> Animal: Polar bears Story	Science>Biology> Animal: Mountain gorillas Story	Social Studies> Cultural anthropology: Amazing ancient cultures of the world Story	Science> Earth science: Clouds and weather Story	
Book 5	Social Studies> Ethics: Rules in daily life Story	Science>Biology: The five senses Report	Social Studies> Cultural anthropology: Astonishing festivals Report	Art>Music: Stories from two operas Story	Social Studies> World culture & history: The Renaissance Story	
Book 6	Social Studies> World geography & travel: Tourist attractions around the world Story	Science>Biology> Animal: Dinosaurs Story	Science> Astronomy: The solar system Story	Social Studies> People: Three great people who overcame hardships Story	Science>Scientific technology: The wonderful world of robots Report	
Book 7				Science & Social Studies> Technology & culture: Inventions from around the world Report	Art>Works of art: Famous paintings Report	
Book 8						
Book 9						
Book 10						

* 10 books in each level will be published.

How to Use This Book

• Before Reading

You can easily find the topic and what kind of story you are about to read.

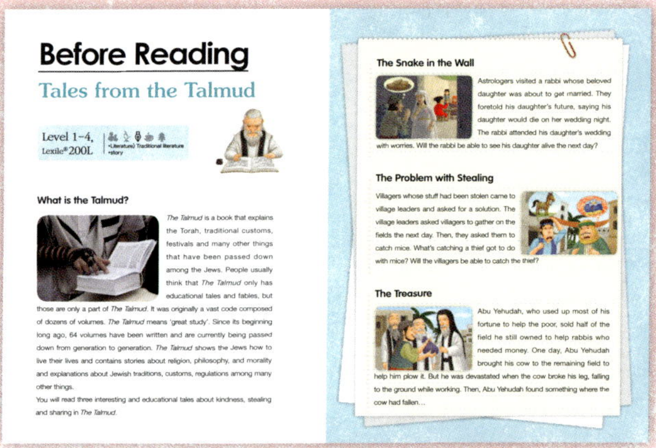

• The text

All the stories were written by professional writers from the U.S. and England, so you will read authentic and appropriate English sentences and expressions in every book in the series.

• Pop Quiz

Check out right away if you understand what you have just read by solving a pop quiz that checks your comprehension.

• Key Words

The key words and expressions on each page are listed for you to easily study them.

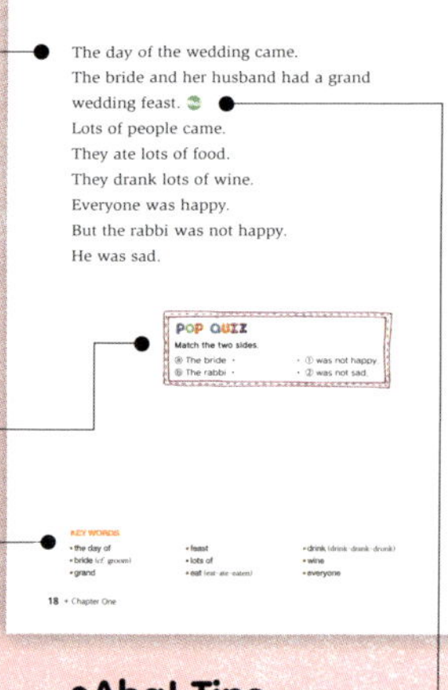

• Aha! Tips

Download free Korean explanations at *www.ihappyhouse.co.kr* for all of the sentences marked with "Aha!". These explain cultural, scientific, and economic knowledge or they deal with aspects of English such as grammatical structures or idiomatic expressions. There are lots of "Aha! Tips" to help you understand the text.

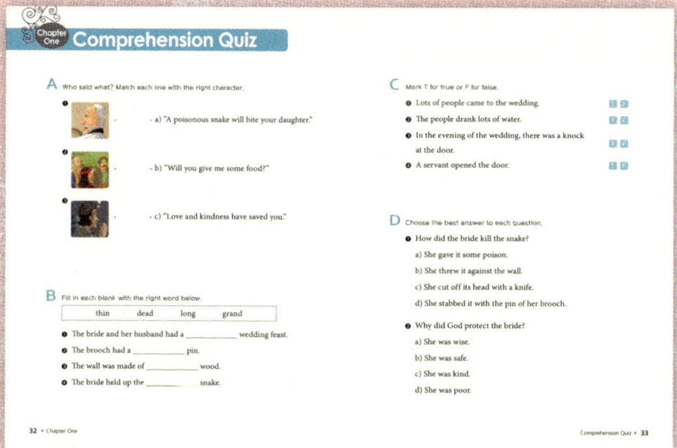

•Comprehension Quiz

After reading one chapter, solve various questions to find out if you fully understand the content.

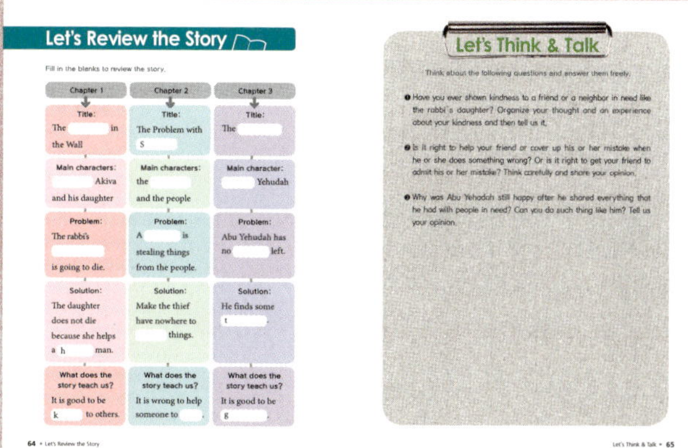

•Let's Review the Story /
•Let's Think & Talk

Fill in the blanks in the organizer to summarize the whole story. Express your own thinking and feelings about the story by answering the questions. You can build up logic and reasoning skills for your essay examinations in the future.

Appendix

Audio CD

In the CD audio book form, the texts are read vividly by American professional voice actors.
(MP3 files downloaded for free)

After-reading Test

Solve an additionally provided After-reading Test for each book.

The Korean translation, Answer Keys, a Word Quiz, a Word List, and Aha! Tips for each book

You can download them for free at *www.ihappyhouse.co.kr*

Before Reading

Tales from the Talmud

Level 1–4,
Lexile® 200L

•Literature〉Traditional Literature
•Story

What is the Talmud?

The Talmud is a book that explains the Torah, traditional customs, festivals and many other things that have been passed down among the Jews. People usually think that *The Talmud* only has educational tales and fables, but those are only a part of *The Talmud*. It was originally a vast code composed of dozens of volumes. *The Talmud* means 'great study'. Since its beginning long ago, 64 volumes have been written and are currently being passed down from generation to generation. *The Talmud* shows the Jews how to live their lives and contains stories about religion, philosophy, and morality and explanations about Jewish traditions, customs, regulations among many other things.

You will read three interesting and educational tales about kindness, stealing and sharing in *The Talmud*.

The Snake in the Wall

Astrologers visited a rabbi whose beloved daughter was about to get married. They foretold his daughter's future, saying his daughter would die on her wedding night. The rabbi attended his daughter's wedding with worries. Will the rabbi be able to see his daughter alive the next day?

The Problem with Stealing

Villagers whose stuff had been stolen came to village leaders and asked for a solution. The village leaders asked villagers to gather on the fields the next day. Then, they asked them to catch mice. What's catching a thief got to do with mice? Will the villagers be able to catch the thief?

The Treasure

Abu Yehudah, who used up most of his fortune to help the poor, sold half of the field he still owned to help rabbis who needed money. One day, Abu Yehudah brought his cow to the remaining field to help him plow it. But he was devastated when the cow broke his leg, falling to the ground while working. Then, Abu Yehudah found something where the cow had fallen…

Contents

Tales from the Talmud

Tales from the Talmud

What Is the Talmud?

The Talmud is a book.

It is a very special book.

It is special to the Jewish people.

It tells them about the wise things
that rabbis talk about. Aha!

Rabbis are Jewish leaders.

They teach people about God.

They teach people how to live good lives.

If two people argue, rabbis decide who is right.

KEY WORDS

- Talmud
- special
- Jewish
- tell (tell-told-told)
- wise
- rabbi
- leader
- teach (teach-taught-taught)
- God
- how to + *Verb*
- lives
- if
- argue
- decide
- right

The Talmud is very old.

It was written hundreds of years ago.

In the Talmud, the Jews can read their special laws.

They can read the wise things that rabbis say.

They can read stories.

The stories tell people how to live their lives. **Aha!**

They are stories about love and wisdom.

They show people how to live a good life.

KEY WORDS

- **be written** (write-wrote-written)
- **hundreds of years ago**
- **Jew**
- **can**
- **law**
- **wisdom**

Love
Wisdom

The Snake in the Wall

There was once a rabbi.

He was called Rabbi Akiva.

He was very wise.

The rabbi had a daughter.

He loved her very much.

The daughter met a young man.

She liked him very much.

He wanted to marry her.

She wanted to marry him.

So a wedding date was set.

"I hope that you will be happy," said the rabbi.

"I hope that your husband will be happy.

I hope that you will be happy together."

KEY WORDS

- snake
- wall
- once
- be called
- **have** (have-had-had)
- daughter
- **meet** (meet-met-met)
- like
- marry
- so
- wedding
- date
- **be set** (set-set-set)
- hope
- **husband** (*cf.* wife)
- together

But some men came to the rabbi.

They were astrologers.

"We can tell what will happen in the future,"
said one of the astrologers.

"Tell me what will happen," said the rabbi.

"What will happen to my daughter?

Will she be happy with her husband?"

"We must tell you something sad," said the
astrologer. Aha!

"Your daughter will die."

The rabbi was shocked.

"How will she die?" he asked.

"A snake will bite her," said the astrologer.

"It will be a poisonous snake."

"When will it happen?" said the rabbi.

"On the evening of her wedding," said the astrologer.

The rabbi was very sad.

He did not want his daughter to die.

But how could he stop it?

There was nothing he could do.

- **come** (come-came-come)
- **astrologer**
- **happen**
- **in the future**
- **must**
- **something**
- **die**
- **shocked**
- **bite** (bite-bit-bitten)
- **poisonous**
- **on the evening of**
- **could**
- **stop**
- **nothing**

The day of the wedding came.

The bride and her husband had a grand

wedding feast. **Aha!**

Lots of people came.

They ate lots of food.

They drank lots of wine.

Everyone was happy.

But the rabbi was not happy.

He was sad.

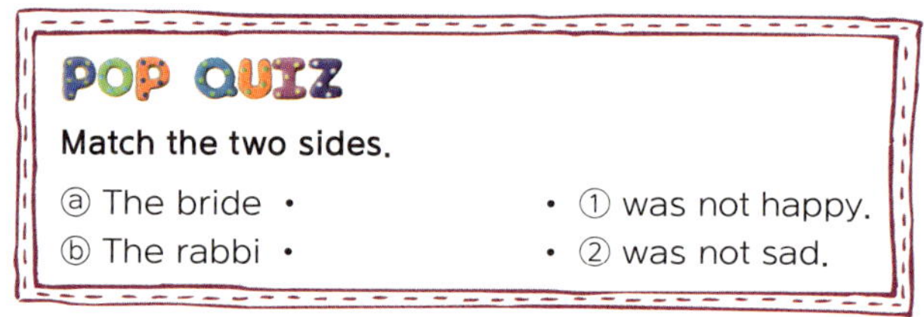

KEY WORDS

- the day of
- bride (*cf.* groom)
- grand
- feast
- lots of
- eat (eat-ate-eaten)
- drink (drink-drank-drunk)
- wine
- everyone

Evening came.

There was a knock at the door. **Aha!**

The bride heard the knock.

She waited for a servant to open the door.

But the servants were too busy.

There was another knock at the door.

The bride heard the knock again.

She waited for a servant to open the door.

But the servants were still too busy.

"I will open the door myself," said the bride.

POP QUIZ

Why did the bride try to open the door herself?

ⓐ She was waiting for someone.
ⓑ The servants were too busy.

- knock
- hear (hear-heard-heard)
- wait
- servant
- too
- busy

- another
- still
- oneself
- get up (get-got-gotten)
- leave (leave-left-left)
- go to see (go-went-gone)

She got up.

She left the table.

She left the grand feast.

She left her new husband.

The bride went to the door.

She went to see who was there.

A man stood at the door.

He was very poor.

He had no food.

His clothes were rags.

"Will you give me some food?" he asked.

"I am very hungry."

"I will get you some food," said the bride.

She went back to the grand feast.

There was no food left.

It had all gone.

But the bride wanted to help the poor man.

So she took her own plate of food.

She took it to the door.

She gave it to the man.

"You may have this food," she said.

"Thank you," said the poor man.

He ate the food.

Then, he went away.

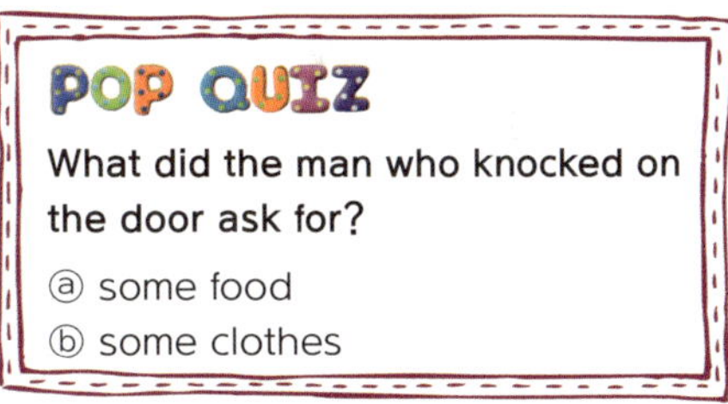

KEY WORDS

- **stand** (stand-stood-stood)
- **poor** (↔ rich)
- **clothes**
- **rag**
- **give** (give-gave-given)
- **hungry** (↔ full)

- **get**
- **go back to**
- **have gone**
- **help**
- **take** (take-took-taken)
- **own**

- **plate**
- **may**
- **then**
- **go away**

Late that night, the feast was over.

The bride and her husband went to their bedroom.

The rabbi stood at the door.

"Be careful," he said to the bride.

She laughed.

"Why should I be careful?

I am with my new husband.

He loves me. I love him.

I am safe with him."

The bride went into the bedroom with her husband.

She took off her wedding clothes.

She took off her brooch.

It had a long pin.

"Where shall I put my brooch?" she said.

"I want to keep it safe.

I do not want to lose it."

"Push the pin into the wall," said her husband.

"The wall is made of wood.

The brooch will stay there.

It will be safe there."

KEY WORDS

- late that night
- be over
- bedroom
- be careful
- laugh
- should

- safe
- into
- take off
- brooch
- pin
- put (put-put-put)

- keep (keep-kept-kept)
- lose (lose-lost-lost)
- push (↔ pull)
- be made of (make-made-made)
- wood
- stay

So the bride went to the wall.

It was made of thin wood.

There was a hollow behind the wall.

She did not know that a snake was hiding
there.

It was a poisonous snake.

The bride pushed the pin into the wall.

The pin was very long.

It went right through the wall.

It went into the eye of the snake.

The pin went right into the head of the snake.

The pin killed the snake.

The bride and her husband slept safely in
their bedroom.

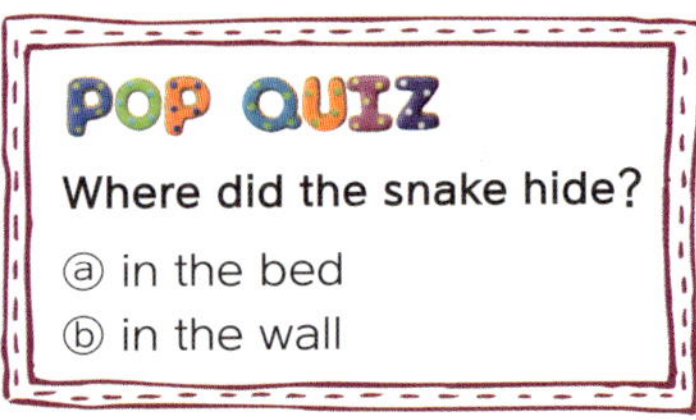

KEY WORDS

- thin
- hollow
- behind

- **know** (know-knew-known)
- **hide** (hide-hid-hidden)
- **through**

- **kill**
- **sleep** (sleep-slept-slept)
- **safely**

The next morning, the rabbi knocked on the door.

"My daughter," he cried.

"Are you awake?"

He was afraid that she was dead.

The bride opened the door.

"Good morning, father," she said.

"I am awake."

"You are alive!" cried the rabbi.

"The astrologers said that you would die.

They said that a snake would bite you.

They said that the snake would kill you."

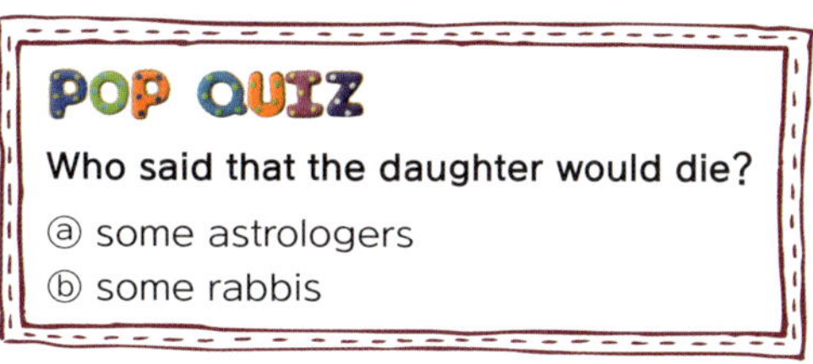

KEY WORDS

▪ cry

▪ awake

▪ afraid

▪ dead (↔ alive)

The bride laughed.

"Here is the snake," she said.

She held up the dead snake.

"God has protected you," said the rabbi.

"You must have done something kind.

God always rewards kindness.

Did you do something kind at your wedding feast?"

"I opened the door," said the bride.

"A poor man was there.

I gave my food to him."

"Love and kindness have saved you," said the rabbi.

"Love saves people from death."

KEY WORDS

- here + *be Verb*
- **hold up** (hold-held-held)
- **protect**
- **kind**
- **always**

- reward
- kindness
- save
- death

Comprehension Quiz

A Who said what? Match each line with the right character.

1 

  • a) "A poisonous snake will bite your daughter."

2 

  • b) "Will you give me some food?"

3 

  • c) "Love and kindness have saved you."

B Fill in each blank with the right word below.

thin	dead	long	grand

1 The bride and her husband had a ______________ wedding feast.

2 The brooch had a ______________ pin.

3 The wall was made of ______________ wood.

4 The bride held up the ______________ snake.

C Mark T for true or F for false.

❶ Lots of people came to the wedding. `T` `F`

❷ The people drank lots of water. `T` `F`

❸ In the evening of the wedding, there was a knock at the door. `T` `F`

❹ A servant opened the door. `T` `F`

D Choose the best answer to each question.

❶ How did the bride kill the snake?

a) She gave it some poison.

b) She threw it against the wall.

c) She cut off its head with a knife.

d) She stabbed it with the pin of her brooch.

❷ Why did God protect the bride?

a) She was wise.

b) She was safe.

c) She was kind.

d) She was poor.

Chapter Two

The Problem with Stealing

People were shouting in the town. Aha!

"My horse is missing!" shouted one man.

"My bag of gold is missing!" shouted another man.

"Where have they gone?
They have been stolen!"

More things went missing.

The people were upset.

They went to the leaders of the town.

"Our things have gone," they said.

"They have been stolen."

"We must do something," said the leaders.

They talked for a long time.

KEY WORDS

- problem
- stealing (*cf.* steal)
- shout
- be[go] missing
- be stolen (steal-stole-stolen)
- more
- upset
- for a long time

At last, they had an idea.

"We will catch the thief.

We will punish him.

He must pay back seven times the amount

that he stole."

The people were glad.

They thought that this was fair.

"My horse is missing," said one man.

"I will get back seven horses."

"My bag of gold is missing," said the other

man.

"I will get back seven bags of gold."

- at last
- have an idea
- catch (catch-caught-caught)
- thief
- punish
- pay back
- times

- amount
- glad
- think (think-thought-thought)
- fair
- get back
- the other
- anyone

- be killed
- helper
- worse
- than
- let (let-let-let)
- explain
- have a meeting

But the leaders had more to say.

"We will catch anyone who helps a thief.

We will punish him.

He will be killed."

The people were shocked.

"Why should the helper be killed?" said one man.

"The thief is worse than the helper," said another man.

"Let me explain," said one of the leaders.

"We will have a meeting."

The meeting was held in a big field.

Everyone was invited.

"Catch some mice," said one leader.

"Catch as many as you can.

Bring them here."

The people were surprised.

But they went away.

They caught some mice.

They caught as many as they could.

They brought the mice to the field.

"Take some wheat.

Put it in front of the mice," said another leader.

"Then, let them go."

So the people took some wheat.

They put it in front of the mice.

Then, they let them go.

The mice took the wheat.

They took it back to their holes.

They hid the wheat in the holes.

They did not come out again that day.

"Now, go home," said the leaders.

So the people went home.

▲ wheat

KEY WORDS

- be held
- be invited
- mice
- as many as + *Subject* + can[could]
- **bring** (bring-brought-brought)
- surprised

- wheat
- in front of
- take back
- hole
- come out

The next day, they came back to the field.

The leaders were there.

"Catch some more mice," they said.

"Catch as many as you can.

Seal up their holes.

Then, bring them here."

The people were surprised.

But they went away.

They caught some mice.

They caught as many as they could.

They sealed up the holes.

They brought the mice to the field.

"Take some wheat.

Put it in front of the mice," said one leader.

"Then, let them go."

So the people took some wheat.

They put it in front of the mice.

Then, they let them go.

The mice took the wheat.

They took it back to their holes.

But they could not get into their holes!

The holes were sealed up.

The mice could not hide the wheat.

They could not eat it all.

So they took the wheat back.

They put it back where it had been.

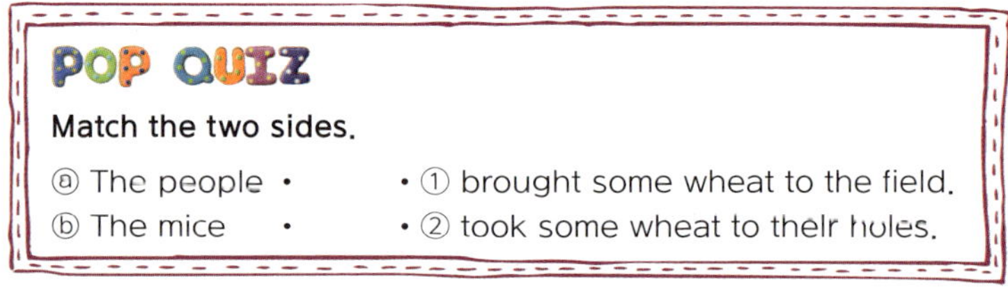

KEY WORDS

▪ put back

"Let me explain," said one of the leaders.

"These mice are like thieves.

They need a safe place to hide things.

If they do not have a safe place, they put the things back.

They do not take any more.

A thief with a friend to help him will hide things.

But a thief without a friend will put the things back.

So we punish the friend who helps the thief.

It is wrong to steal. Aha!

But it is also wrong to *help* someone to steal."

KEY WORDS

- thieves
- need
- place
- any more
- without
- wrong

A Circle the characters which said each line.

❶ "We must do something." **PEOPLE / LEADERS**

❷ "Our things have gone." **PEOPLE / LEADERS**

B Fill in each blank with the right word below.

upset	glad	surprised	shocked

❶ The people were ____________ when the leaders wanted to punish the thief.

❷ The people were ____________ when the leaders wanted to kill the helper.

❸ The people were ____________ when the leaders told them to catch mice.

❹ The people were ____________ when their things were stolen.

C Mark T for true or F for false.

❶ The meeting was held in a big church. T F

❷ Everyone was invited to the meeting. T F

❸ The people had to catch some thieves. T F

❹ The mice are like thieves. T F

 Choose the best answer to each question.

❶ Who did the leaders want to punish?

a) the horse and the thief

b) the thief and his helper

c) the people and their children

d) the mice and the horse

❷ Why did the mice bring the wheat back the second time?

a) They were not hungry.

b) They could not put it in their holes.

c) They did not want any more wheat.

d) They were sorry that they had taken it.

E Put the sentences in order.

❶ The mice hid the wheat in their holes.

❷ The people put some wheat in front of the mice.

❸ The mice took the wheat to their holes.

❹ The mice did not come out again that day.

________ → ________ → ________ → ________

Chapter Three

The Treasure

Once there was a man called Abu Yehudah.

He was very generous.

He gave money to people who needed it. **Aha!**

It did not matter who they were.

It did not matter where they came from.

If they needed help, Abu Yehudah gave it to them.

One day, some rabbis came to his city.

They needed some money.

They knew that Abu Yehudah was generous.

They hoped that he would give them some money.

KEY WORDS

- treasure
- called
- generous
- matter
- come from
- one day
- city
- stay away from

But now Abu Yehudah was poor.

He did not have much money.

It had all gone.

"I want to help the rabbis," he said.

"But I cannot.

I will stay away from the city.

I do not want to meet them."

Abu Yehudah had a wife.

"What is wrong?" she said.

"You look sad. Why are you sad?"

"I do not want to meet the rabbis.

I want to help them," he said.

"But I have no money so I cannot."

"Yes, you can," said his wife. Aha!

"You can help them.

We still have a field.

You can sell half of it."

"That is a good idea," he said.

"I will sell half of the field.

I will keep the other half.

Then, I can still grow things and I can also

help the rabbis."

KEY WORDS

- **sell** (sell-sold-sold)
- **half**
- **grow** (grow-grew-grown)

sell

So Abu Yehudah rushed out of the house.

He sold half of his field.

He got some money for it.

He took the money to the city.

He gave it to the rabbis.

"Here is some money!" he said.

"I am sorry there is not much.

I hope you will take it.

I hope it will help you."

The rabbis took his money.

They thanked him for it.

They prayed to God.

"Please bless Abu Yehudah," they said. Aha!

"He is a generous man."

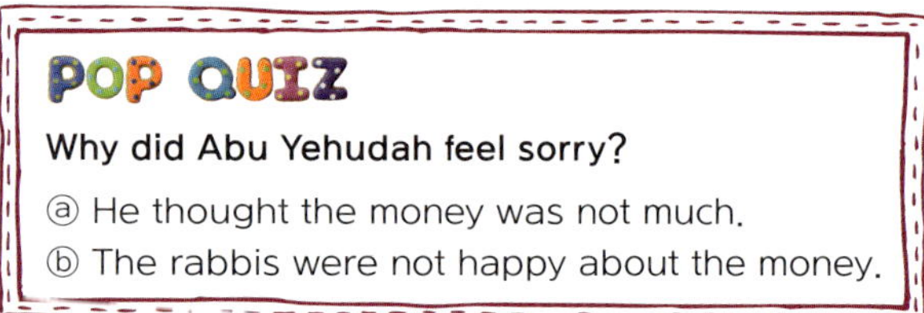

KEY WORDS

- rush out of
- for
- thank for
- pray
- bless

Abu Yehudah went home.

He had a very small field and one cow left.

He took the cow and went to his field.

He wanted to plow the field.

The cow began to pull the plow.

But the cow fell!

It hurt its leg.

The leg was broken.

"Oh no!" cried Abu Yehudah.
"What shall I do now? Everything is going wrong.
I cannot plow my field.
I cannot plant my crops.
I cannot grow any food."
He was very sad.
"God has not blessed me," he said.

POP QUIZ

Why did Abu Yehudah plow the field?

ⓐ He wanted to grow things.
ⓑ He wanted to find treasure.

- plow
- **begin** (begin-began-begun)
- **fall** (fall-fell-fallen)
- **hurt** (hurt-hurt-hurt)
- **be broken** (break-broke-broken)

- shall
- everything
- go wrong
- plant
- crop

Abu Yehudah tried to help the cow.

He put a shovel under it.

He tried to lift it up.

But the cow was heavy.

He could not lift it.

He did not give up.

He put the shovel under the cow again.

The shovel went into the ground.

It hit something in the ground.

It made a sound like metal.

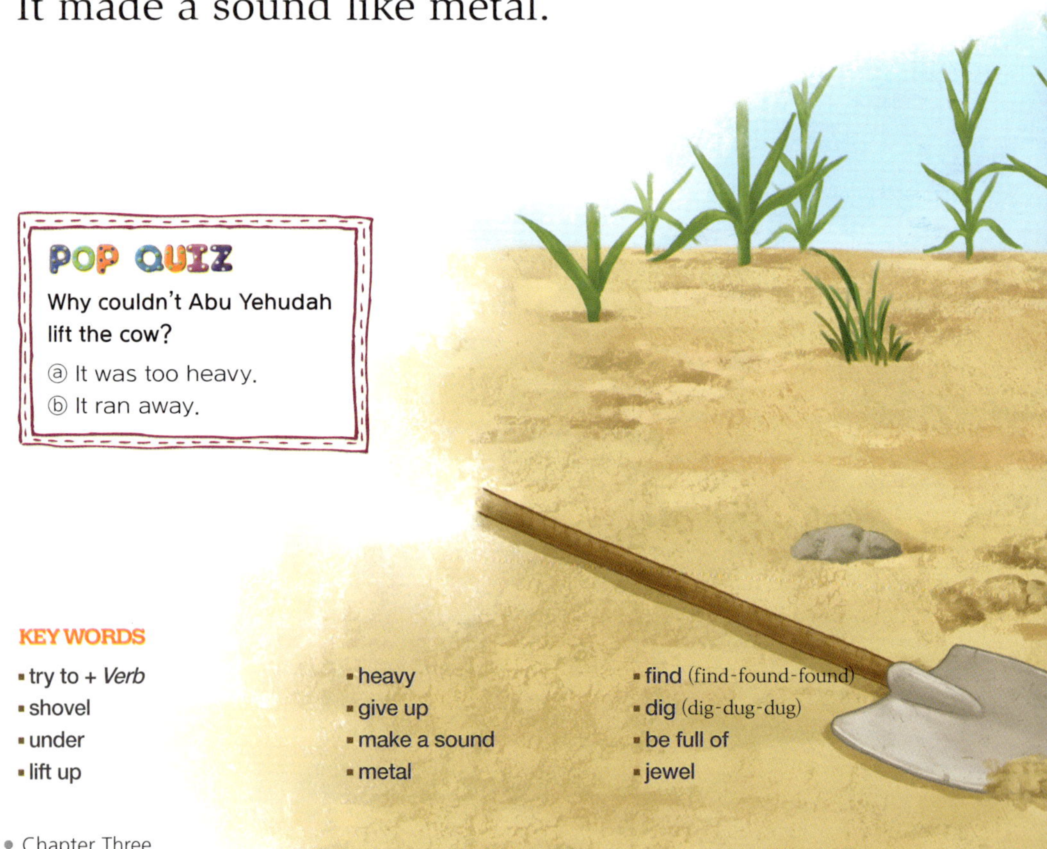

POP QUIZ

Why couldn't Abu Yehudah
lift the cow?

ⓐ It was too heavy.
ⓑ It ran away.

KEY WORDS

- try to + *Verb*
- shovel
- under
- lift up

- heavy
- give up
- make a sound
- metal

- find (find-found-found)
- dig (dig-dug-dug)
- be full of
- jewel

"What is that?" cried Abu Yehudah.

"I have found something."

He began to dig.

There was a hole.

The hole was full of gold.

The hole was full of silver.

The hole was full of jewels.

KEY WORDS
- amazed
- a lot of (= lots of)
- pick up
- carry

Abu Yehudah was amazed.

"There is a lot of treasure here," he said.

"I am glad that the cow fell.

It helped me to find the treasure."

He picked up the gold.

He picked up the silver.

He picked up the jewels.

He carried all the treasure back home.

"Come here!" he shouted to his wife.

"Look what I have found!

God has blessed us."

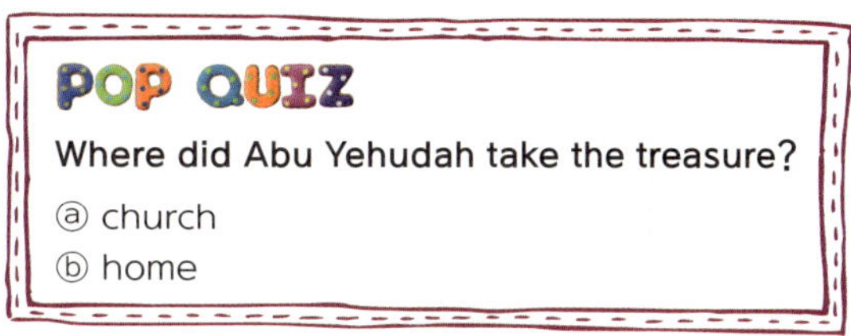

Abu Yehudah was rich again.

He bought some houses.

He bought some fields.

He bought some land to grow fruit.

But he was very generous.

He gave money to people who needed it.

He was glad because he could give more money.

- **buy** (buy-bought-bought)
- because
- this time
- even when

One day, the rabbis came back to the city.
Abu Yehudah ran to meet them.
He took lots of money with him.
"I can give you more money this time!" he
said.
"God has blessed me so much."
"It is because you are a generous man," said
one of the rabbis.
"Even when you had no money, you still
wanted to help people."

A Who said what? Match each line with the right character.

❶ 

❷ 

❸ 

a) "You can sell half of your field."

b) "It is because you are a generous man."

c) "God has blessed us."

B Put the sentences in order.

❶ Abu Yehudah took his money to the city.

❷ Abu Yehudah sold half of his field.

❸ Abu Yehudah gave the money to the rabbis.

❹ Abu Yehudah got some money for the field.

________ → ________ → ________ → ________

 Choose the best answer to each question.

❶ Why did Abu Yehudah NOT want to meet the rabbis at first?

a) He did not like them.

b) He did not live near the city.

c) He did not want to give them any money.

d) He did not have much money to give to them.

❷ What did Abu Yehudah want to do with the other half of his field?

a) He wanted to keep cows on it.

b) He wanted to hide treasure under it.

c) He wanted to grow things on it.

d) He wanted to give it to his wife.

D Mark T for true or F for false.

❶ Abu Yehudah used a horse to plow his field. 

❷ The cow fell in the field. T F

❸ Abu Yehudah broke his leg. T F

❹ The hole was full of jewels. T F

Let's Review the Story

Fill in the blanks to review the story.

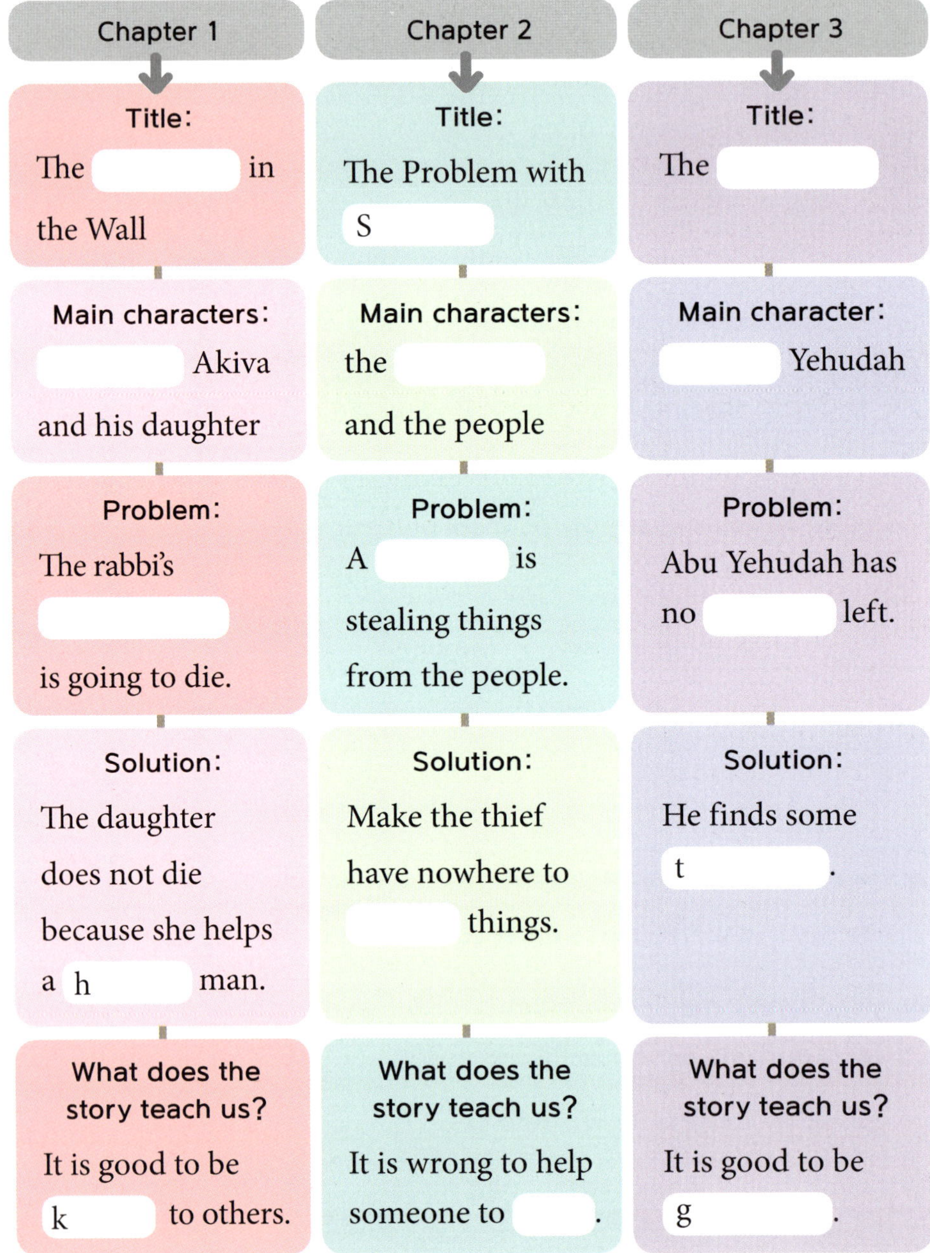

Let's Think & Talk

Think about the following questions and answer them freely.

❶ Have you ever shown kindness to a friend or a neighbor in need like the rabbi's daughter? Organize your thoughts about being kind to others, and then make notes about one experience. Now, tell it to us.

❷ Is it right to help your friend or cover up his or her mistake when he or she does something wrong? Or is it right to get your friend to admit his or her mistake? Think carefully and share your opinion.

❸ Why was Abu Yehudah still happy after he shared everything that he had with people in need? Can you do such thing like him? Tell us your opinion.

Let's Review the Story

Chapter 1	Chapter 2	Chapter 3
Title: The `Snake` in the Wall	**Title:** The Problem with `Stealing`	**Title:** The `Treasure`
Main characters: `Rabbi` Akiva and his daughter	**Main characters:** the `leaders` and the people	**Main character:** `Abu` Yehudah
Problem: The rabbi's `daughter` is going to die.	**Problem:** A `thief` is stealing things from the people.	**Problem:** Abu Yehudah has no `money` left.
Solution: The daughter does not die because she helps a `hungry` man.	**Solution:** Make the thief have nowhere to `hide` things.	**Solution:** He finds some `treasure`.
What does the story teach us? It is good to be `kind` to others.	**What does the story teach us?** It is wrong to help someone to `steal`.	**What does the story teach us?** It is good to be `generous`.

Smart Readers: **Wise** & **Wide**

After-reading Test

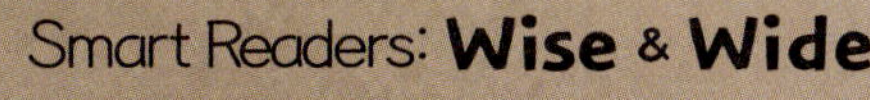

• Tales from the Talmud

• Level 1

• 18 Questions

(Vocabulary 5 / Reading Comprehension 10 /

Sentence Structure & Grammar 3)

1. Which of the following pair has the wrong past tense form of the listed verb?
    ① set – set   ② put – put
    ③ let – let   ④ meet – meet

2. Which of the following has the right plural noun?
    ① life → lifes
    ② mouse → mouses
    ③ thief → thieves
    ④ horse → horsees

3. Which is a pair of words that are opposites?
    ① bride ↔ daughter
    ② safe ↔ happy
    ③ dead ↔ alive
    ④ jewel ↔ gold

4. What is the correct word for the blank?

    > The hole was full __________ gold.

    ① of   ② to
    ③ on   ④ in

5. Which of the following word has the meaning below?

    > someone who can tell what is going to happen in the future

    ① husband   ② astrologer
    ③ servant   ④ thief

6. When was the Talmud written?
   ① a few years ago
   ② ten years ago
   ③ hundreds of years ago
   ④ thousands of years ago

7. What kinds of stories are in the Talmud?
   ① danger and death
   ② fun and adventure
   ③ love and wisdom
   ④ space and stars

8. Why was the rabbi sad in the first story?
   ① He did not want his daughter to die.
   ② He did not want his daughter to marry.
   ③ He did not want his daughter to grow up.
   ④ He did not want his daughter to eat bad food.

9. Who knocked at the door in the first story?
   ① a servant
   ② the astrologer
   ③ the bride
   ④ a poor man

10. Which two of these were stolen in the second story?
    ① silver   ② gold
    ③ a horse   ④ a cow

11. What animal did the people catch in the second story?
    ① dogs   ② mice
    ③ cows   ④ cats

12. Which of these things was NOT in the hole in the third story?
　① gold
　② fruit
　③ jewels
　④ silver

13. What was the first thing that Abu Yehudah did with the treasure?
　① He hid it in the ground again.
　② He showed it to his wife.
　③ He gave it all to the rabbis.
　④ He bought some houses with it.

14. What did NOT Abu Yehudah do?
　① He carried the treasure back home.
　② He dug a hole in the ground.
　③ He showed the treasure to the rabbis.
　④ He bought some land to grow fruit.

15. What is NOT right about Abu Yehudah?
　① He was very generous.
　② He always wanted to help people.
　③ He was sad because he should give more money away.
　④ In the end, he was rich again.

※ Choose the wrong part of the sentence. (16~17)

16.
We <u>must</u> <u>to tell</u> <u>you</u> <u>something sad</u>.
　　① 　　② 　　③ 　　　④

17.
<u>"Let me to explain,"</u> <u>said</u> one of the leaders.
① ②   ③   ④

18. What is the right sentence?
    ① There be a knock at the door.
    ② There was a knock at the door.
    ③ A knock at the door be here.
    ④ A knock at the door were there.

✛ You can download the answer keys at www.ihappyhouse.co.kr

Sarah J. Dodd
Sarah J. Dodd is an experienced primary school teacher who resides in the UK, but has also lived and taught in Australia. She has a PhD in Science and a certificate in Creative Writing. She has published several books for children: "An Angel Anyway" (Anyway Press, 2008) the "Little Angels" series (Lion Children's Books, 2009/10), "The Lion Picture Bible" (Lion Children's Books, 2015) and "Legs: the tale of a meerkat lost and found" (Lion Children's Books, 2015). Her poetry for children has also been highly commended and published in the anthology "Let in the Stars" (Manchester Metropolitan University, 2014).
She is currently working on further picture books for the very young, and a novel for older children.

Tales from the Talmud

Retold by Sarah J. Dodd
Illustrated by Changjun Lee

First Published in May 2015
Second Printing September 2019

Editorial Manager: Juyon Choi
Editors: Kyunghee Jang, Jiyeong Park
Designer: Eunhee Lee
Cover Designer: Eunhee Lee

Published and distributed by

201, 43-2, Poeun-ro 2ga-gil, Mapo-gu, Seoul, Korea 04026
Tel: 82-2-6494-1455   Fax: 82-2-6494-1465
Homepage: www.ihappyhouse.co.kr
Publisher: Kyudo Chung

Copyright © Darakwon Publishing Company 2015
English Edition published 2015, by arrangement with Darakwon, by Happy House
English Edition Copyright © 2015, Happy House

All rights reserved. No part of this publication may be reproduced, stored in a retrieval system, or transmitted in any form or by any means, electronic, mechanical, photocopying or otherwise, without the prior consent of the copyright owner. Refund after purchase is possible only according to the company regulations. Contact the above telephone number for any inquiries. Consumer damages caused by loss, damage, etc. can be compensated according to the consumer dispute resolution standards announced by the Korea Fair Trade Commission. An incorrectly collated book will be exchanged.

ISBN: 978-89-6653-190-5 18740 / 978-89-6653-156-1 18740(set)

[Components]
• 1 Audio CD (Recording Studio: Aram)
• Answer Keys & Korean Translation: Free download at www.ihappyhouse.co.kr